Instant Vortex Cookbook

Easy and Delicious Dishes to Make with Your Air Fryer. How to Stay Healthy without Guilt

Stefanie Cruz

© Copyright 2021 - All rights reserved.

Table of contents

BREAKFAST AND BRUNCH

1. Blueberry Cobbler

Preparation Time: 5 minutes

Cooking Time: 15 minutes

Servings: 4

Ingredients:

- ⅓ cup whole-wheat pastry flour
- ¾ teaspoon baking powder
- Dash sea salt
- ½ cup fresh blueberries
- ¼ cup Granola, or plain store-bought granola
- ½ cup 2% milk

- 2 tablespoons pure maple syrup

- ½ teaspoon vanilla extract

- Cooking oil spray

Directions:

- In a medium bowl, whisk the baking powder, flour, and salt. Add the milk, maple syrup, and vanilla and gently whisk, just until thoroughly combined.

- Preheat the unit by selecting BAKE, setting the temperature to 350 degrees F, and setting the time to three minutes Select START.

- Spray a 6-by-2-inch round baking pan with cooking oil and pour the batter into the pan. Top evenly with the blueberries and granola.

- Once the unit is preheated, place the pan into the basket.

- Select BAKE, set the temperature to 350 degrees F, and set the time to fifteen minutes Select START to begin.

- When the cooking is complete, the cobbler should be nicely browned and a knife inserted into the middle should come out clean. Enjoy topped with a little vanilla yogurt.

Nutrition: Calories 112 Fat 1g Carbs 23g Protein 3g

2. Grilled Ham and Cheese

Preparation Time: 5 minutes

Cooking Time: 10 minutes

Servings: 2

Ingredients:

- 1 teaspoon butter

- Four slices bread

- Four slices smoked country ham

- Four slices Cheddar cheese

- Four thick slices tomato

Directions:

- Spread ½ teaspoon of butter onto one side of 2 slices of bread. Each sandwich will have one slice of bread with butter and one slice without.

- Assemble each sandwich by layering two slices of Cheddar, two slices of ham, and two slices of tomato on the unbuttered pieces of bread. Top with the other bread slices, buttered side up.

- Place the sandwiches in the oven buttered-side down. Cook for four minutes

- Open the air fryer. Flip the grilled cheese sandwiches. Bake for an additional four minutes

- Cool before serving. Cut each sandwich in half.

Nutrition: Calories 525 Fat 25g Carbs 34g Protein 41g

BREAD, PIZZA AND PASTA

3. Baked Bread

Preparation Time: 1hr 15 m

Cooking Time: 50 minutes

Servings: 1

Ingredients:

- Three Eggs

- 250 g low fat quark

- 30 g Green grain meal, wheat meal or oat meal

- 11/2 teaspoon ammonium bicarbonate

- 11/2 teaspoon salt

- Bread spice mix

- 1 teaspoon honey

- 100 g Spelled flour, possibly more

- 70 g Psyllium or flax seeds

- 30 g Poppy

- 1 teaspoon Vinegar

- 50g Sunflower seeds

Directions:

- Mix all the ingredients in sequence using an electric beater with a dough hook. If the mixture is flaky, take it out and knead again. Form an even loaf and bake in the air fryer at 165 degrees C for fifty minutes.

Nutrition: Calories: 299 Fat: 11 g Carbs: 20 g

4. Pizza

Preparation Time: 5 minutes

Cooking Time: 8 minutes Serving: 1

Ingredients:

- Two large eggs

- ¼ cup unsweetened, unflavored almond milk

- ¼ teaspoon acceptable sea salt

- ¼ cup shredded Parmesan cheese

- Six pepperoni slices

- 1/8 teaspoon ground black pepper

- ¼ cup diced onions

- ¼ teaspoon dried oregano leaves

- ¼ cup pizza sauce, warmed, for serving

Directions:

- Preheat the air fryer to 350 degrees F. Grease a six by 3-inch cake pan.

- In a bowl, use a fork to whisk together the almond milk, eggs, salt, and pepper. Add the onions and stir to mix. Pour the mixture into the greased pan—top with the cheese, oregano and pepperoni slices. Cook for eight minutes, until the eggs are cooked to your liking.

- Loosen the eggs from the pan's sides with a spatula and place them on a serving plate. Drizzle the pizza sauce on top.

Nutrition: Calories 357; Fat 25g; Carbs 9g;

5. Vegan Beer Bread

Preparation time: 10 minutes

Cooking time: 45 minutes

Servings: 4

Ingredients:

- 225 g wheat flour

- 150 ml dark beer or malt beer

- 75 g sourdough

- 10 g yeast

- tbsp. salt

- For the rye sourdough:

- 75 g rye flour

- 75 ml water

Direction:

- Mix rye flour and lukewarm water into a dough and cover and leave to rest in a warm place for twelve hours.

- As soon as the sourdough is left to rest, dissolve the yeast and salt in 3 tbsp. Of dark beer until bubbles form. Then add the sourdough, wheat flour and the remaining dark beer and knead for eight minutes.

- Cover again the dough and then let it rest in a warm place for 1-2 hours. Then either put the dough in the hot air fryer's baking pan without further processing or shape it like a loaf and place it on the grid insert. Cook bread for 5 minutes at 390° F, then reduce the baking temperature to 390° F and bake for another twenty-five minutes.

- Now and then, brush the bread with a little water to have excellent, shiny crust forms.

Nutrition: Calories: 326 kcal Fat: 1.31 g Carbs: 67.31 g

6. Chicken & Pepperoni Pizza

Preparation Time: 20 minutes

Cooking Time: 30 minutes   Servings: 2

Ingredients:

- 2 cups cooked chicken, cubed
- 20 slices pepperoni
- 1 cup sugar-free pizza sauce
- 1 cup mozzarella cheese, shredded
- ¼ cup parmesan cheese, grated

Directions:

- Place the chicken into the base of a four-cup baking dish and add the pepperoni and pizza sauce on top. Stir well to coat the meat with the sauce thoroughly.
- Add the parmesan and mozzarella on top of the chicken, then place the baking dish into your fryer.
- Cook for fifty minutes at 375 degrees F.
- When everything is bubbling and melted, remove from the oven.

7. Meat Lovers' Pizza

Preparation: 10 min Cooking: 12 minutes Serving: 2

Ingredients:

- 1pre-prepared 7-inch pizza crust, defrosted if necessary.

- 1/3 cup of marinara sauce. 2ounces of grilled steak, sliced into bite-sized pieces 2ounces of salami, cut fine

- 2ounces of pepperoni, cut fine

- ¼ cup of American cheese

- ¼ cup of shredded mozzarella cheese

Directions:

- Preheat the Air Fryer Oven to 350° F. Lay the pizza dough flat on a sheet of parchment paper or tin foil, cut large enough to hold the entire pie crust but small enough that it will leave the edges of the air fryer basket uncovered to allow for air circulation.

- Using a fork, stab the pizza dough several times across the surface – piercing the pie crust will allow air to circulate throughout the crust and ensure even cooking.

With a deep soup spoon, scoop the marinara sauce onto the pizza dough, and spread evenly in expanding circles over the pie-crust surface.

- Be sure to leave at least 1/2 inch of bare dough around the edges to ensure that extra-crispy crunchy first bite of the crust! Distribute the steak pieces and the slices of salami and pepperoni evenly over the sauce-covered dough, then sprinkle the cheese in an even layer on top.

- Set the air fryer timer to twelve minutes, and place the pizza with foil or paper on the fryer's basket surface. Again, be sure to leave the edges of the basket uncovered to allow for proper air circulation, and don't let your bare fingers touch the hot surface. After twelve minutes, when the Air Fryer Oven shuts off, the cheese should be perfectly melted and lightly crisped, and the pie crust should be golden brown. If necessary, using a spatula – or two, remove the pizza from the air fryer basket and set on a serving plate. Wait a few minutes until the pie is cool enough to handle, then cut into slices.

8. Mozzarella, Bacon & Turkey Calzone

Preparation Time: 20 minutes

Cooking Time: 10 minutes

Servings: 4

Ingredients:

- Pizza dough
- 4 oz cheddar cheese, grated
- 1 oz mozzarella cheese
- 1 oz bacon, diced
- 2 cups cooked and shredded turkey
- One egg, beaten
- 1 teaspoon thyme
- 4 tablespoon tomato paste
- 1 teaspoon basil
- 1 teaspoon oregano
- Salt and pepper

Directions:

1. Preheat the Air fryer oven to 350° F.

2. Divide the pizza dough into 4 equal pieces so you have the dough for 4 small pizza crusts. Combine the tomato paste, oregano, basil, and thyme, in a bowl.

3. Brush the mixture onto the crusts just make sure not to go all the way and avoid brushing near the edges on one half of each crust, place 1/2 turkey, and season the meat with some salt and pepper.

4. Top the meat with some bacon. Combine the cheddar and mozzarella and divide it between the pizzas, making sure that you layer only one half of the dough.

5. Brush the edges of the crust with the beaten egg. Fold the crust and seal with a fork. Cook for ten minutes.

Nutrition: Calories 435.4 Fat 15.6g Carbs 53.6g

9. Pita Bread

Preparation time: 10 minutes

Cooking time: 15 minutes

Servings: 4

Ingredients:

- 1 tbsp. Pizza sauce

- 1 Pita bread

- 25 cup Mozzarella cheese

- Olive oil

- 1 Stainless-steel short-legged trivet

- 7 slices Pepperoni

- 5 tsp. Fresh minced garlic

- 25 cup Sausage

- 1 tbsp. Thinly sliced onions

Directions:

- Heat the Air Fryer in advance to 350 degrees F.

- Spoon the sauce onto the bread.

- Mince the garlic and thinly slice the onions. Toss on the toppings using a drizzle of oil.

- Arrange it in the Air Fryer and place the trivet.

- Set the timer for 6 minutes. Serve when it's nicely browned.

Nutrition: Calories: 374 Cal Carbs: 57 g Fat: 4 g.

SNACKS AND APPETIZERS

10. Air Fryer Walnuts

Preparation Time: 10 Minutes

Cooking Time: 5 minutes

Servings: 6

Ingredients:

- 2 cups walnuts

- 1 teaspoon olive oil

- Salt and Pepper

Directions:

- Add walnuts, oil, pepper, and salt into the bowl and toss well.

- Add walnuts to the air fryer basket then place an air fryer basket in baking pan.

- Place a baking pan on the oven rack. Set to air fry at 350 degrees F for five minutes.

Nutrition: Calories 264 Fat 25.4 g Carbs 4.1 g

11. Avocado Chips

Preparation Time: 10 minutes

Cooking time: 10 minutes

Servings: 3

Ingredients:

- One avocado, pitted, peeled and sliced

- Salt and pepper

- ½ cup vegan bread crumbs

- A drizzle of olive oil

Directions:

- In a bowl, mix bread crumbs with salt and pepper and mix.

- Brush avocado slices with the oil, coat them in bread crumbs, place them in your air fryer's basket and cook at the temperature of 390 degrees F for ten minutes, shaking halfway.

- Divide into bowls

Nutrition: Calories 180 Fat 11g Carbs 7g

12.   Allspice Chicken Wings

Preparation Time:

Cooking Time: 45 minutes

Serving: 8

Ingredients:

- ½ tsp celery salt

- ½ tsp bay leaf powder

- ¼ tsp allspice

- 2 pounds chicken wings

- ½ tsp ground black pepper

- ½ tsp paprika

- ¼ tsp dry mustard

- ¼ tsp cayenne pepper

Directions:

- Grease the air fryer basket and preheat to 340 degrees F. In a bowl, mix celery salt, bay leaf powder, paprika, dry mustard, black pepper, cayenne pepper, and all spice. Coat the wings thoroughly in this mixture.

- Arrange the wings in an even layer in the air fryer basket. Cook the chicken until it's no longer pink around the bone, for thirty minutes then, increase the temperature to 380 degrees F and cook for six minutes more, until crispy on the outside.

Nutrition: Calories 332 Fat 10.1 g Carbs 31.3 g

13. Avocado Rolls

Preparation Time: 20 minutes

Cooking Time: 25 minutes

Servings: 5

Ingredients:

- Ten rice paper wrappers

- Three avocados, sliced

- One tomato, diced

- Salt and pepper

- 1 tbsp. olive oil

- 4 tbsp. sriracha

- 2 tbsp. sugar

- 1 tbsp. rice vinegar

- 2 tbsp. sesame oil

Directions:

- Mash avocados in a bowl.

- Toss in the tomatoes, salt and pepper.

- Mix well.

- Arrange the rice paper wrappers.

- Scoop mixture on top.

- Roll and seal the edges with water.

- Cook in the air fryer at 350° F for 5 minutes.

- Mix the rest of the ingredients.

Nutrition: Calories 422 Saturated Fat 5.8g Carbs 38.7g

MAINS

14. Breaded Mushrooms

Preparation time: 15 minutes

Cooking time: 7 minutes

Servings: 2

Temperature: 360degreesF

Ingredients:

- ½ pound button mushrooms

- One cup almond meal

- 1 Flax-Egg

- 1 cup almond flour

- 3 ounces cashew cheese

- Salt

- Pepper

Directions:

- Preheat and set the Air Fryer's temperature to 360 degrees F

- Take a shallow bowl and toss almond meal with cheese into it

- Whisk flax egg in one bowl and spread flour in another

- Wash mushrooms, then pat dry

- Coat every mushroom with flour

- Dip each of them in the flax egg first, then in breadcrumb

- Spray with cooking oil and place back in the Air Fryer

- Air fry these mushrooms for 7 minutes

- Toss the mushrooms after 3 minutes

Nutrition: Calories: 140 Fat: 9.2g Carbs: 6.9g

15. Bang Panko Breaded Fried Shrimp

Preparation Time: 5 Minutes

Cooking Time: 8 Minutes

Servings: 4

Ingredients:

- One teaspoon paprika   Montreal chicken seasoning
- One egg white   ½ cup almond flour
- ¾ cup panko bread crumbs
- 1 pound raw shrimp (peeled and deveined)

Bang Bang Sauce:

- ¼ cup sweet chili sauce
- 2 tablespoon sriracha sauce
- 1/3 cup plain Greek yogurt

Directions:

- Ensure your Air Fryer is preheated to 400 degrees. Season all shrimp with seasonings. Add flour to one bowl, egg white in another, and breadcrumbs to a third.

- Dip seasoned shrimp in flour, then egg whites, and then breadcrumbs. Spray coated shrimp with olive oil and add to air fryer basket. Set temperature to 400°F, and set time to 4 minutes. Cook 4 minutes, flip, and cook an additional 4 minutes.

- To make the sauce, mix together all sauce ingredients until smooth.

Nutrition: Calories 212 Carbs 12g Fat 1g

16.   Basil Chicken Bites

Preparation Time: 10 minutes

Cooking Time: 30 minutes

Serving: 4

Ingredients:

- 1 1/2 lb. chicken breasts, skinless; boneless and cubed

- 1/2 cup chicken stock

- 2 tsp. smoked paprika

- Salt and pepper

- 1/2 tsp. basil; dried

Directions:

- In a pan that fits the air fryer, combine all the ingredients, toss, introduce the pan in the fryer and cook at 390°F for 25 minutes

- Divide between plates and serve for lunch with a side salad.

Nutrition: Calories: 22; Fat: 12g Carbs: 5g Protein: 13g

POULTRY

17. Basil-Garlic Breaded Chicken Bake

Preparation Time: 5 minutes

Cooking Time: 30 minutes

Serving: 2

Ingredients:

- 2 boneless skinless chicken breast halves (4 ounces each)
- 1 tablespoon butter, melted
- 1 large tomato, seeded and chopped
- 2 garlic cloves, minced
- 1 1/2 tablespoons minced fresh basil

- 1/4 cup all-purpose flour

- 1/4 cup egg substitute

- 1/4 cup grated Parmesan cheese

- 1/4 cup dry bread crumbs

- 1/4 teaspoon pepper

- 1/2 teaspoon salt

- 1/2 tablespoon olive oil

Directions:

- In a shallow bowl, whisk OK egg substitute and place flour in a separate bowl—dip chicken in flour, then egg, and then flour. In a small bowl, whisk OK butter, bread crumbs, and cheese. Sprinkle over chicken.

- Lightly grease the baking pan of the air fryer with cooking spray. Place breaded chicken on the bottom of the pan. Cover with foil.

- For 20 minutes, cook at 390°F.

- Meanwhile, in a bowl, whisk well-remaining ingredient.

- Remove foil from pan and then pour over chicken the remaining Ingredients.

- Cook for 8 minutes.

Nutrition: Per Serving: Calories: 311; Fat: 11g; Protein: 31g; Carbs: 22g

18. BBQ Chicken Wings

Preparation Time: 10 Minutes

Cooking Time: 55 minutes

Servings: 8

Ingredients:

- 32 chicken wings
- 1 1/2 cups BBQ sauce
- Salt and pepper
- 1/4 cup olive oil

Directions:

- Line baking sheet with parchment paper and set aside.
- Select bake, set temperature 375 F, timer for 55 minutes. Press start to preheat the oven.
- In a mixing bowl, toss chicken wings with olive oil, pepper, and salt.
- Arrange chicken wings on a baking sheet and bake for 50 minutes.

- Toss chicken wings with BBQ sauce and bake for 5 minutes more.

Nutrition: Calories 173 Fat 8.3 g Carbs 17 g Protein 7.4 g

19. BBQ Spicy Chicken Wings

Preparation Time: 10 Minutes

Cooking Time: 45 minutes Servings: 6

Ingredients:

- 3 lbs. chicken wings

- 2 tbsp olive oil

- 1/2 cup BBQ spice rub

Directions:

- Select bake, set temperature 390 F, timer for 45 minutes. Press start to preheat the oven.

- Brush chicken wings with olive oil and place in a large mixing bowl.

- Add BBQ spice over chicken wings and toss until well coated.

- Arrange chicken wings on rack in a single layer and bake for 45 minutes.

Nutrition: Calories 483 Fat 22.2 g Carbs 1.5 g Protein 65.8 g

20. Baked Chicken

Preparation Time: 5minutes

Cooking time: 45 minutes

Servings: 6

Ingredients:

- 1/2 cup butter

- 1tsp. pepper

- 3tbsp. garlic, minced

- 1whole chicken

Directions:

- Pre-heat your fryer at 350°F.

- Allow the butter to soften at room temperature, then mix well in a small bowl with the pepper and garlic.

- Massage the butter into the chicken. Any remaining butter can go inside the chicken.

- Cook the chicken in the fryer for half an hour. Flip, then cook on the other side for another thirty minutes.

- Test the temperature of the chicken by sticking a meat thermometer

- the fat of the thigh to make sure it has reached 165°F. Take care when removing the chicken from the fryer. Let sit for ten minutes before you carve it.

21.   Buffalo Chicken Wings

Preparation Time: 5 minutes

Cooking Time: 30 minutes

Serving: 8

Ingredients:

- 1-2 tbsp. brown sugar

- 1 tbsp. Worcestershire sauce

- 1/2 C. butter

- 1/2 C. cayenne pepper sauce

- 4 pounds of chicken wings

- 1 tsp. salt

Directions:

- Whisk salt, brown sugar, Worcestershire sauce, butter, and hot sauce together and set aside.

- Dry wings and add to the air fryer basket.

- Set temperature to 380°F, and set time to 25 minutes. Cook was tossing halfway through.

- When the timer sounds, shake wings, bump up the temperature to 400 degrees, and cook another 5 minutes.

- Take out wings and place them into a big bowl. Add sauce and toss well.

- Serve alongside celery sticks.

Nutrition: Calories: 402; Fat: 16g; Protein: 17g

22. Buffalo Chicken Tenders

Preparation Time: 15 minutes

Cooking Time: 10 minutes

Servings: 2

Ingredients:

- One egg 1 cup mozzarella cheese, shredded
- ¼ cup feta cheese
- ¼ cup buffalo sauce
- 1 cup cooked chicken, shredded

Directions:

- Combine all ingredients (except for the feta). Line the basket of your fryer with a suitably-sized piece of parchment paper. Lay the mixture into the fryer and press it into a circle about half an inch thick. Crumble the feta cheese over it. Cook for 8 minutes at 400°F. Turn the fryer off and allow the chicken to rest inside before removing it with care.
- Cut the mixture into slices.

RED MEAT

23. Lamb Kebabs

Servings: 3

Preparation Time: 10 Minutes

Cooking Time: 60 Minutes

Ingredients:

- 1 ½ pounds lamb shoulder, bones removed and cut into pieces
- Two tablespoons cumin seeds, toasted
- Two teaspoons caraway seeds, toasted
- One tablespoon Sichuan peppercorns
- One teaspoon sugar
- Two teaspoons crushed red pepper flakes

- Salt and pepper

Directions:

- Place all ingredients in bowl and allow the meat marinate in the refrigerator for at least two hours.
- Preheat the air fryer to 390 degrees F.
- Grill the meat for fifteen minutes per batch.
- Flip the meat every eight minutes for even grilling.

Nutrition: Calories: 465; Carbs: 7.7g; Protein: 22.8g; Fat: 46.9g

SEAFOOD

24. Baked Salmon Spring Rolls

Preparation Time: 20minutes

Cooking time: 8 minutes

Servings: 4

Ingredients:

- 1/2 pound (227 g) salmon fillet

- 1 teaspoon toasted sesame oil

- 1 onion, sliced

- 1 carrot, shredded

- 1 yellow bell pepper, thinly sliced

- 1/3 cup chopped fresh flat-leaf parsley

- ¼ cup chopped fresh basil

- 8 rice paper wrappers

Directions:

- Arrange the salmon in the air fry basket. Drizzle the sesame oil all over the salmon and scatter the onion on top.

- Select Air Fry, set temperature to 370°F, and set time to 10 minutes. Select Start to begin preheating.

- Once preheated, place the basket on the air fry mode.

- Meanwhile, fill a small shallow bowl with warm water. One by one, dip the rice paper wrappers into the water for a few seconds or until moistened, then put them on a work surface.

- When cooking is complete, the fish should flake apart with a fork. Remove from the oven to a plate.

- Make the spring rolls: Place 1/8 of the salmon and onion mixture, parsley, carrot, bell pepper, and basil into the rice wrapper's center and fold the sides over the filling. Roll up the wrapper carefully and tightly like you would a burrito. Repeat with the remaining wrappers and filling.

- Transfer the rolls to the air fry basket.

- Select Bake, set temperature to 380°F, and set time to 8 minutes. Select Start to begin preheating.

- Once preheated, place the basket on the bake position.

- When cooking is complete, the rolls should be crispy and lightly browned. Remove from the oven and cut each roll in half, and serve warm.

25. Blackened Mahi

Preparation Time: 10 minutes

Cooking Time: 17 minutes

Servings: 4

Ingredients:

- Four Mahi fillets
- 1 tsp. paprika
- 1 tsp. garlic powder
- 3 tbsps. Olive oil
- 1/2 cayenne
- 1 tsp. oregano
- 1 tsp. cumin
- 1 tsp. onion powder
- 1/2 tsp. pepper
- 1/2 tsp. salt

Directions:

- Line the Baking Pan with foil and set aside.
- Place fish fillets on the baking pan and drizzle with oil.

- In a small bowl, mix together cumin, onion powder, cayenne, paprika, oregano, garlic powder, pepper, and salt.

- Rub fish fillets with a spice mixture.

- Set to Bake at 450 degrees F for 12 minutes.

Nutrition: Calories 189 Fat 12 g Carbs 2 g Protein 19 g

Cajun Catfish Fillets

Preparation Time: 15 minutes

Cooking Time: 20 minutes

Servings: 4

Ingredients:

- lb. catfish fillets, cut ½-inch thick
- 3/4 tsp. chili powder
- tsp. crushed red pepper
- tsp. onion powder
- 1/2 tsp. ground cumin
- tbsps. dried oregano, crushed
- Salt and Pepper

Directions:

- Line the Baking Pan with foil and set aside.
- In a bowl, mix cumin, crushed red pepper, chili powder, onion powder, oregano, pepper, and salt.
- Rub fish fillets with the spice mixture on both sides.
- Place fish fillets in a baking pan.

- Set to Bake at 350 degrees F for 15 minutes.

Nutrition: Calories 165 Fat 9 g Carbs 2 g Protein 18 g

26. Cajun Salmon

Preparation Time: 12 minutes

Cooking Time: 8 minutesServings: 2

Ingredients:

- 2 (4-oz.) salmon fillets, skin removed

- 2 tbsp. Unsalted butter; melted.

- 1 tsp. Paprika

- 1/8 tsp. Ground cayenne pepper

- ¼ tsp. Ground black pepper

- ½ tsp. Garlic powder

Directions:

- Brush each fillet with butter. Combine remaining ingredients: in a small bowl and then rub onto fish. Place fillets into the air fryer basket

- Adjust the temperature to 390 Degrees F and set the timer for 7 minutes. When fully cooked, the internal temperature will be 145 Degrees F.

Nutrition: Calories: 253; Protein: 29g; Fat: 16g; Carbs: 4g

VEGETABLES

27. Baby Potatoes

Preparation Time: 10 minutes

Cooking Time: 20 minutes

Serve: 2

Ingredients:

- 12 oz. baby potatoes
- 1/2 tbsp. olive oil
- 1/4 tsp. paprika
- 1/4 tsp. chili powder
- 1/4 tsp. cumin
- 1/4 tsp. garlic salt

- 1/4 tsp. pepper

- 1/2 tsp. kosher salt

Directions:

- Add all ingredients into a zip-lock bag and shake well.

- Transfer baby potatoes into the air fryer basket.

- Place air fryer basket into the oven and select air fry mode with 370 degrees F for twenty minutes. Toss wice.

Nutrition: Calories 133 Fat 3.8 g Carbs 22 g Protein 4.6 g

SOUPS

28. Bean Soup

Preparation Time: 35 minutes

Cooking Time: 30 minutes

Servings: 4

Ingredients:

- One onion, chopped

- One large carrot, chopped

- Two garlic cloves, minced

- 15 oz. can white beans, rinsed and drained

- 1 cup spinach leaves, trimmed and washed

- cups chicken broth

- 1 tablespoon. Paprika

- 1 tablespoon. Dried mint

- Tablespoon. Extra virgin olive oil

- salt and black pepper, to taste

Directions:

- Heat the olive oil over medium heat and gently sauté the onion, garlic, and carrot.

- Add in beans, broth, salt, and pepper and bring to a boil.

- Reduce heat and cook for 10 minutes, or until the carrots are tender. Stir in spinach, and simmer for about 5 minutes, until spinach is wilted.

DESSERTS

Pineapple Bites

Preparation Time: 10 minutes

Cooking Time: 10 minutes Servings: 4

Ingredients:

- ½ of pineapple ¼ cup desiccated coconut

- One tablespoon fresh mint leaves, minced

- 1 cup vanilla yogurt

Directions:

- Remove the outer skin of the pineapple and cut into long 1-2 inch thick sticks.

- In a dish, place the coconut.

- Coat the pineapple sticks with coconut evenly.

- Select the "Air Fry" and set the cooking time to 10 minutes.

- Set the temperature at 390 degrees F.

- Arrange the pineapple sticks in a lightly greased "Air Fry Basket" and insert it in the oven.

- Meanwhile, for a dip in a bowl, mix mint and yogurt.

- Serve pineapple sticks with yogurt dip.

Nutrition: Calories 124 Fat 2.6 g Carbs 21.6 g Protein 4.4 g

29.   Cheesecake Bites

Preparation Time: 20 minutes

Cooking Time: 2 minutes

Servings: 12

Ingredients:

- 8 oz. cream cheese, softened

- ½ cup plus two tablespoons sugar, divided

- Four tablespoons heavy cream, divided

- ½ teaspoon vanilla extract

- ½ cup almond flour

Directions:

- In the bowl of a stand mixer fitted with the paddle attachment, add cream cheese, ½ cup sugar, two tablespoons heavy cream, and vanilla extract and beat until smooth.

- Using a paddle attachment, pour the mixture onto a baking sheet lined with baking paper.

- Freeze for about 30 minutes or until firm.

- In a small bowl, place the remaining cream.

- In another bowl, add the almond flour and remaining sugar and mix well.

- Dip each cheesecake bite into the cream and then top with the flour mixture.

- Select the "Air Fry" mode and set the baking time to 2 minutes on your oven.

- Set the temperature to 300 degrees F.

- Place pan in "Air Fry Basket" and place in the oven.

Nutrition: Calories 149 Fat 10.7 g Carbs 11.7 g Protein 2.5 g

FRUITS

30. Cocoa and Coconut Bars (Vegan)

Preparation time: 10 minutes

Cooking time: 14 minutes

Servings: 12

Ingredients:

- 6 ounces coconut oil, melted

- Three tbsp. Flax meal combined with three tbsp. water

- 3 ounces of cocoa powder

- Two tsp. vanilla

- ½ tsp. baking powder

- 4 ounces coconut cream

- Five tbsp. coconut sugar

Directions:

- In a blender, mix the flax meal with oil, vanilla, cream, cocoa powder, baking powder, and sugar and pulse.

- Pour this into a lined baking dish that fits your air fryer, introduce in the fryer at 320 degrees F, bake for 14 minutes, slice into rectangles and serve.

Nutrition: Calories 178 Fat 14g Carbs 12g Protein 5 g

DIABETIC RECIPES

31. Chicken Tenders

(Prep Time: 10 minutes| Cook Time:20 minutes| Servings: 3)

Ingredients

- Chicken tenderloins: 4 cups

- Eggs: one

- Superfine Almond Flour: ½ cup

- Powdered Parmesan cheese: ½ cup

- Kosher Sea salt: ½ teaspoon

- (1-teaspoon) freshly ground black pepper

- (1/2 teaspoon) Cajun seasoning,

Instructions

- On a small plate, pour the beaten egg.

- Mix all ingredients in a ziploc bag. Almond flour freshly ground black pepper & kosher salt and other seasonings.

- Spray the air fryer with oil spray.

- To avoid clumpy fingers with breading and egg. Use different hands for egg and breading. Dip each tender in egg and then in bread until they are all breaded.

- Using a fork to place one tender at a time. Bring it in the ziploc bag and shake the bag forcefully. make sure all the tenders are covered in almond mixture

- Using the fork to take out the tender and place it in your air fryer basket.

- Spray oil on the tenders.

- Cook for 12 minutes at 350F, or before 160F registers within. Raise temperature to 400F to shade the surface for 3 minutes. Serve with sauce.

Nutritional value: per serving: Calories 280 |Proteins 20g |Carbs 6g|Fat 10g |Fiber 5g

32. Kale & Celery Crackers

(Prep time: 10 min| Cooking time: 20 min| Servings: 6)

Ingredients

- One cups flax seed, ground

- 1 cups flax seed, soaked overnight and drained

- 2 bunches kale, chopped1 bunch basil, chopped

- ½ bunch celery, chopped2 garlic cloves, minced

- 1/3 cup olive oil

Instructions

- Mix the ground flaxseed with the celery, kale, basil, and garlic in your food processor and mix well.

- Add the oil and soaked flaxseed, then mix again, scatter in the pan of your air fryer, break into medium crackers and cook for 20 minutes at 380 degrees F.

- Serve as an appetizer and break into cups.

Nutritional Value: per serving: calories 143|fat 1g| fiber 2g| carbs 8g| Protein 4g

Diabetic Turkey Recipes

33. No-breaded Turkey Breast

(Prep Time: 5 minutes| Cook Time:55 minutes| Servings: 10)

Ingredients

- Turkey breast: 4 pounds, ribs removed, bone with skin

- Olive oil: 1 tablespoon Salt: 2 teaspoons

- Dry turkey seasoning (without salt): half tsp.

Instructions

- Rub half tbsp of olive oil over turkey breast. Sprinkle

  salt, turkey seasoning on both sides of turkey breast

with half tbsp of olive oil.

- Let the air fryer preheat at 350 F. put turkey skin side down in air fryer and cook for 20 minutes until the turkey's temperature reaches 160 F for half an hour to 40 minutes.
- Let it sit for ten minutes before slicing.
- Serve with fresh salad.

Nutritional value: per serving: Calories: 226kcal| Protein: 32.5g|Fat: 10g|carbs 22 g

Diabetic Fish & Seafood Recipes

34. Crispy Fish Sticks in Air Fryer

(Prep Time: 10 minutes| Cook Time:15 minutes | Serving 4)

Ingredients

- Whitefish such as cod 1 lb.

- Mayonnaise ¼ c

- Dijon mustard 2 tbsp.

- Water 2 tbsp.

- Pork rind 1&1/2 c

- Cajun seasoning ¾ tsp

- Kosher salt& pepper to taste

Instructions

- Spray non-stick cooking spray to the air fryer rack.

- Pat the fish dry & cut into sticks about 1 inch by 2 inches' broad

- Stir together the mayo, mustard, and water in a tiny small dish. Mix the pork rinds & Cajun seasoning into another small container.

- Adding kosher salt& pepper to taste (both pork rinds & seasoning can have a decent amount of kosher salt, so you can dip a finger to see how salty it is).

- Working for one slice of fish at a time, dip to cover in the mayo mix & then tap off the excess. Dip into the mixture of pork rind, then flip to cover. Place on the rack of an air fryer.

- Set at 400F to Air Fry & bake for 5 minutes, then turn the fish with tongs and bake for another 5 minutes. Serve.

Nutritional value: per serving: Cal: 263| Fat: 16g| Net Carbs: 1g| Protein: 26.4g

35. Honey-Glazed Salmon

(Prep Time: 10 minutes| Cook Time:15 minutes| Servings: 2)

Ingredients

- Gluten-free Soy Sauce: 6 tsp

- Salmon Fillets: 2 pcs

- Sweet rice wine: 3 tsp

- Water: 1 tsp

- Honey: 6 tbsp.

Instructions

- In a bowl, mix sweet rice wine, soy sauce, honey, and water.

- Set half of it aside.

- In the half of it, marinate the fish and let it rest for two hours.

- Let the air fryer preheat to 180 C

- Cook the fish for 8 minutes, flip halfway through and cook for another five minutes.

- Baste the salmon with marinade mixture after 3 or 4 minutes.

- The half of marinade, pour in a saucepan reduce to half, serve with a sauce.

Nutritional value: per serving: calories 254| carbs 9.9 g| fat 12 g| protein 20 g|

Diabetic Pork Recipes

36. Pork Tenderloin with Mustard Glazed

(Prep Time: 10 minutes| Cook Time:18 minutes| Servings: 4)

Ingredients

- Yellow mustard: ¼ cup

- One pork tenderloin

- Salt: ¼ tsp

- Honey: 3 Tbsp.

- Freshly ground black pepper: ⅛ tsp

- Minced garlic: 1 Tbsp.

- Dried rosemary: 1 tsp

- Italian seasoning: 1 tsp

Instructions

- With a knife, cut the top of pork tenderloin. Add garlic (minced) in the cuts. Then sprinkle with kosher salt and pepper.

- In a bowl, add honey, mustard, rosemary, and Italian seasoning mix until combined. Rub this mustard mix all over pork.

- Let it marinate in the refrigerator for at least two hours.

- Put pork tenderloin in the air fryer basket. Cook for 18-20 minutes at 400 F. with an instant-read thermometer internal temperature of pork should be 145 F

- Take out from the air fryer and serve with a side of salad.

Nutritional value: per serving: Calories: 390 | Carbohydrates: 11g | Protein: 59g | Fat: 11g |

Diabetic Beef Recipes

37. Air Fried Beef Schnitzel

(Prep Time: 10 minutes| Cook Time:15 minutes| Servings: 1)

Ingredients

- One lean beef schnitzel

- Olive oil: 2 tablespoon

- Breadcrumbs: ¼ cup

- One egg

- One lemon, to serve

Instructions

- Let the air fryer heat to 180 C.

- In a big bowl, add breadcrumbs and oil, mix well until forms a crumbly mixture

- Dip beef steak in whisked egg and coat in breadcrumbs mixture.

- Place the breaded beef in the air fryer and cook at 180C for 15 minutes or more until fully cooked through.

- Take out from the air fryer and serve with the side of salad greens and lemon.

Nutrition Value: per serving: Calories 340 |Proteins 20g |Carbs 14g |Fat 10g |Fiber 7g

Diabetic Chicken Recipes

38. Lemon Rosemary Chicken

(Prep Time: 30 minutes| Cook Time:20 minutes| Servings: 2)

Ingredients

For marinade

- Chicken: 2 and ½ cups Ginger: 1 tsp, minced

- Olive oil: 1/2 tbsp. Soy sauce: 1 tbsp.

For the sauce

- Half lemon

- Honey: 3 tbsp.

- Oyster sauce: 1 tbsp.

- Fresh rosemary: half cup, chopped

Instructions

- In a big mixing bowl, add the marinade ingredients with chicken, and mix well.

- Keep in the refrigerator for at least half an hour.

- Let the oven preheat to 200 C for three minutes.

- Place the marinated chicken in the air fryer in a single layer. And cook for 6 minutes at 200 degrees.

- Meanwhile, add all the sauces ingredients in a bowl and mix well except for lemon wedges.

- Brush the sauce generously over half-baked chicken add lemon juice on top.

- Cook for another 13 minutes at 200 C. flip the chicken halfway through. Let the chicken evenly brown.

- Serve right away and enjoy.

Nutrition Value: per serving: Calories 308 |Proteins 25g |Carbs 7g|Fat 12 g |

39. Air Fryer Chicken & Broccoli

(Prep Time: 10 minutes| Cook Time:15 minutes| Servings: 4)

Ingredients

- Olive oil: 2 Tablespoons

- Chicken breast: 4 cups, bone and skinless (cut into cubes) Half medium onion, roughly sliced

- Low sodium soy sauce: 1 Tbsp.

- Garlic powder: half teaspoon Rice vinegar: 2 teaspoons

- Broccoli: 1-2 cups, cut into florets

- Hot sauce: 2 teaspoons Fresh minced ginger: 1 Tbsp.

- Sesame seed oil: 1 teaspoon Salt & black pepper, to taste

Instructions

- In a bowl, add chicken breast, onion, and broccoli. Combine them well.

- In another bowl, add ginger, oil, sesame oil, rice vinegar, hot sauce, garlic powder, and soy sauce mix it well. Then add the broccoli, chicken, and onions to marinade.

- Coat well the chicken with sauces. And let it rest in the refrigerator for 15 minutes

- Place chicken mix in one even layer in air fryer basket and cook for 16-20 minutes, at 380 F. halfway through, toss the basket gently and cook the chicken evenly

- Add five minutes more, if required.

- Add salt and pepper, if needed.

- Serve hot with lemon wedges.

Nutritional   value: per   serving:
Calories 191|Fat 7g|Carbohydrates 4g|Protein 25g

Diabetic Desserts Recipes

40. Sugar-Free Air Fried Carrot Cake

(Prep Time: 15 minutes| Cook Time: 40 minutes| Servings: 8)

Ingredients

- All-Purpose Flour: 1 ¼ cups

- Pumpkin Pie Spice: 1 tsp

- Baking Powder: one teaspoon

- Splenda: 3/4 cup

- Carrots: 2 cups–grated

- 2 Eggs

- Baking Soda: half teaspoon

- Canola Oil: ¾ cup

Instructions

- Let the air fryer preheat to 350 F. spray the cake pan with oil spray.

- And add flour over that.

- In a bowl, combine the baking powder, flour, pumpkin pie spice, and baking soda.

- In another bowl, mix the eggs, oil, and sugar alternative. Now combine the dry to wet ingredients.

- Add half of the dry ingredients first mix and the other half of the dry mixture.

- Add in the grated carrots.

- Add the cake batter to the greased cake pan.

- Place the cake pan in the basket of the air fryer.

- Let it Air fry for half an hour, but do not let the top too brown.

- If the top is browning, add a piece of foil over the top of the cake.

- Air fry it until a toothpick comes out clean, 35-40 minutes in total.

- Let the cake cool down before serving.

Nutritional Value: Cal 287 | Carbohydrates: 19g | Protein: 4g | Fat: 22g |

30-Day Meal Plan

This meal is designed to help you achieve the best health possible. Hope you enjoy these delicious recipes that will keep your belly full and glucose level under control for days to come.

Week 1

Monday (Day 1)

Breakfast: Bell Peppers Frittata

Lunch: Lemon Rosemary Chicken

Snack: Air-Fryer Kale Chips with dipping

Dinner: Air Fryer Pork Taquitos

Tuesday (Day 2)

Breakfast: Air Fryer Crisp Egg Cups

Lunch: Air-Fried Rosemary Garlic Grilled Prawns

Snack: Air Fryer Buffalo Cauliflower with dipping

Dinner: Air Fried Empanadas

Wednesday (Day 3)

Breakfast: Asparagus Frittata

Lunch: Crispy Air Fryer Fish

Snack: Air Fryer Onion Rings with dipping

Dinner: Air Fryer Lemon Garlic Shrimp

Thursday (Day 4)

Breakfast: Mushroom Oatmeal

Lunch: Chicken Fajitas

Snack: Air Fryer Chicken Nuggets

Dinner: Sriracha & Honey Tossed Calamari

Friday (Day 5)

Breakfast: Air Fryer Egg Rolls

Lunch: Air Fryer Delicata Squash

Snack: Zucchini Parmesan Chips

Dinner: Air Fryer Crispy Fish Sandwich

Saturday (Day 6)

Breakfast: Air Fryer Salmon cakes

Lunch: Air Fryer Popcorn Chicken

Snack: Zucchini Gratin

Dinner: Air Fryer Lemon Pepper Shrimp

Sunday (Day 7)

Breakfast: Air Fryer Egg Rolls

Lunch: Air Fryer Crispy Fish Sticks

Snack: One Blueberry Muffin

Dinner: Air-Fried Buttermilk Chicken

Week 2

Monday (Day 8)

Breakfast: Air-Fried Spinach Frittata

Lunch: Crispy Air Fryer Brussels Sprouts

Snack: Slice of Vegan Cake

Dinner: Air Fryer Turkey Breast

Tuesday (Day 9)

Breakfast: Mushroom Omelet

Lunch: Coconut Shrimp

Dinner: Juicy Turkey Burgers with Zucchini

Wednesday (Day 10)

Breakfast: Mushroom Oatmeal

Lunch: Air Fryer Fish and Chips

Snack: Slice of Berry Cheesecake

Dinner: Air Fryer Meatloaf

Thursday (Day 11)

Breakfast: Lemon-Garlic Tofu

Lunch: Air Fryer Hamburger

Snack: Slice of Carrot Cake

Dinner: Air-Fried Buttermilk Chicken

Friday (Day 12)

Breakfast: Air-fryer omelet

Lunch: Air Fried Empanadas

Snack: Zucchini Chips

Dinner: Air Fry Rib-Eye Steak

Saturday (Day 13)

Breakfast: Breakfast Bombs

Lunch: Orange Chicken Wings

Snack: Low Carb Pork Dumplings with Dipping Sauce

Dinner: Air Fryer Chicken & Broccoli

Sunday (Day 14)

Breakfast: Air-fryer baked eggs

Lunch: Air Fryer Low Carb Chicken Bites

Snack: Half Sugar Free Brownie

Dinner: Air-Fried Turkey Breast with Maple Mustard Glaze

Week 3

Monday (Day 15)

Breakfast: Crisp egg cups

Lunch: Sweet potato fries

Snack: One Apple Cider Donut

Dinner: Air Fryer Whole Wheat Crusted Pork Chops

Tuesday (Day 16)

Breakfast: Vegan Breakfast Sandwich

Lunch: Air Fryer Delicata Squash

Snack: Air Fryer Kale Chips

Dinner: Air-Fried Chicken Pie

Wednesday (Day 17)

Breakfast: Vegan mashed potato bowl

Lunch: Chicken Fajitas

Snack: One blueberry muffin

Dinner: Garlic Parmesan Crusted Salmon

Thursday (Day 18)

Breakfast: Toad in the hole tarts

Lunch: Air Fryer Low Carb Chicken Bites

Snack: Avocado fries

Dinner: Air Fryer Hamburger

Friday (Day 19)

Breakfast: Breakfast bombs

Lunch: Air Fryer Chicken & Broccoli

Snack: Onion rings

Dinner: Air Fryer Sesame Seeds Fish Fillet

Saturday (Day 20)

Breakfast: Mushroom Omelet

Lunch: Garlic Parmesan Crusted Salmon

Snack: Roasted corn

Dinner: Chicken Fajitas

Sunday (Day 21)

Breakfast: Avocado Egg Rolls

Lunch: Air Fryer Lemon Pepper Shrimp

Snack: Zucchini Parmesan Chips

Dinner: Air Fry Rib-Eye Steak

Week 4

Monday (Day 22)

Breakfast: Apple fritter

Lunch: Air-Fried Rosemary Garlic Grilled Prawns

Dinner: Mustard Glazed Air Fryer Pork Tenderloin

Tuesday (Day 23)

Breakfast: Lemon-Garlic Tofu

Lunch: Air Fryer Turkey Breast Tenderloin

Snack: Small slice of sugar-free berry cheesecake

Dinner: Air Fryer Lemon Pepper Shrimp

Wednesday (Day 24)

Breakfast: Vegan Breakfast Sandwich

Lunch: Air Fryer Chicken & Broccoli

Snack: Slice of Carrot Cake

Dinner: Air-Fried Rosemary Garlic Grilled Prawns

Thursday (Day 25)

Breakfast: Egg Air-Fryer Omelet

Lunch: Air Fryer Southwest Chicken

Snack: Air-fry Brownie

Dinner: Air Fryer Sesame Seeds Fish Fillet

Friday (Day 26)

Breakfast: Slice of eggless and vegan cake

Lunch: Air Fryer Low Carb Chicken Bites

Snack: Kale chips

Dinner: Air Fryer Turkey Breast Tenderloin

Saturday (Day 27)

Breakfast: Bell Pepper Frittata

Lunch: Air-Fried Buttermilk Chicken

Snack: Chicken Nuggets

Dinner: Air Fry Rib-Eye Steak

Sunday (Day 28)

Breakfast: Air-fryer Spanakopita Bites

Lunch: Orange Chicken Wings

Snack: One peanut butter cookie

Dinner: Air Fryer Hamburger

Week 5

Monday (Day 29)

Breakfast: Toad in the hole Tart

Lunch: Crab cakes

Snack: Air Fryer Roasted Corn

Dinner: Air Fried Empanadas

Tuesday (Day 30)

Breakfast: Banana muffin with coffee

Lunch: Lemon Rosemary Chicken

Snack: Egg rolls

Dinner: Air Fryer Delicata Squash

CPSIA information can be obtained
at www.ICGtesting.com
Printed in the USA
BVHW091018190421
605287BV00002B/169